D0765708

INSIDE FIGHTER PLANES

Thanks to the creative team:
Senior Editor: Alice Peebles
Fact Checking: Tom Jackson
Illustrations: Mat Edwards and Victor Mclindon
Picture Research: Nic Dean
Design: www.collaborate.agency

Hungry Tomato®
A division of Lerner Publishing Group, Inc.
241 First Avenue North
Minneapolis, MN 55401 USA

For reading levels and more information, look up
this title at www.lernerbooks.com.

Main body text set in Avenir Next Condensed Medium 11/15.
Typeface provided by Linotype AG.

Library of Congress Cataloging-in-Publication Data

Names: Oxlade, Chris.
Title: Inside fighter planes / Chris Oxlade.
Description: Minneapolis : Hungry Tomato, [2018] | Series: Inside
military machines | Includes index.
Identifiers: LCCN 2017006581 (print) | LCCN 2017008472
(ebook) | ISBN 9781512432275 (lb : alk. paper) | ISBN
9781512449990 (eb pdf)
Subjects: LCSH: Fighter planes–History–Juvenile literature.
Classification: LCC UG1242.F5 O93 2018 (print) | LCC UG1242.
F5 (ebook) | DDC   623.74/64–dc23

LC record available at https://lccn.loc.gov/2017006581\

Manufactured in the United States of America
1-41782-23543-3/29/2017

INSIDE FIGHTER PLANES

A "Flying Bedstead," used for experimenting with vertical takeoff in the 1950s

by Chris Oxlade

HUNGRY TOMATO®

Minneapolis

The Supermarine Spitfire was one of the best fighter planes of World War II.

Contents

BATTLE MACHINES: FIGHTER PLANES

Modern fighter planes are superfast, superloud, and supercomplex battle machines, crammed with clever technology. Fighter planes battle each other to control the air because **air superiority** gives one side a big advantage in a conflict. Most modern fighters also have other roles such as attacking enemy forces on the ground.

Fighter Types

These days, the term *fighter* can mean several different kinds of planes, which complete different missions. Many planes can be changed to do different jobs.

Air superiority fighter: A fighter designed to fight enemy aircraft and gain control of the air

Strike fighter: A fighter that also attacks ground targets

Multirole combat aircraft: A fighter that performs various roles, including **air-to-air** combat

Old and New

Two types of aircraft here show how the technology of fighters has changed over the last one hundred years! Above right is a Sopwith **Triplane** from World War I (1914–1918), the first war to feature fighter planes. Below left and right is a Lockheed Martin F-22 Raptor, a modern fighter. Its structure, engine, controls, and weapons would be unrecognizable to a Sopwith Triplane pilot.

F-22 Raptor

The Lockheed Martin F-22 Raptor is a state-of-the-art air superiority fighter. It is fast, agile, and **stealthy**, with air-to-air and **air-to-ground** weapons.

Sopwith Triplane

The Sopwith had only one seat and three sets of wings. It was a favorite among pilots for its ability to move quickly and smoothly.

FIRST FIGHTERS

The first successful powered planes flew in the early years of the twentieth century. World War I began just a decade later, in 1914. Armies on both sides realized that planes would help them see enemy positions. So the first military planes were scout planes. It wasn't long before these planes were armed with machine guns and went on missions to hunt down enemy scouts. The fighter plane was born.

Airco DH. 2

Length: 25 feet (7.7 meters)

Wingspan: 28 feet (8.6 m)

Weight: 943.5 pounds (428 kilograms)

Engine: Gnome rotary

Top speed: 93 miles (150 kilometers) per hour

Top height: 13,993 feet (4,265 m)

Weapons: 1 Lewis gun

Number built: 453

First flight: July 1915

Pusher Planes

Many of the first fighters had a propeller at the back, behind the cockpit, as in this Airco DH. 2. The planes were called pushers because the propeller pushed them along. This layout allowed the pilot to sit in the front of the **fuselage** and fire his gun forward without hitting the propeller.

cylinders spin around, making the propeller spin

crankshaft

piston

Rotary Power

The **rotary engine** was the most popular engine for fighter planes in World War I. A rotary engine was a type of piston engine, in which pistons moved up and down in cylinders. In most engines, the cylinders stay still, and the pistons turn a crankshaft. But in a rotary engine, the crankshaft stays still and the cylinders and pistons spin around with the propeller.

The Wright Flyer

Orville and Wilbur Wright's Flyer made the first controlled, powered flight in the United States in 1903. Before this, flights had been in gliders (with no engines), or just short, uncontrolled hops.

Balloon Attacks

Before and during World War I, armies sent observers up in gas-filled observation balloons to spy on enemy positions. These balloons were an easy target for fighter planes, which could shoot holes in the balloons. The balloons often caught fire as they sank to the ground.

WORLD WAR I ADVANCES

As World War I continued, both sides designed and built better and better fighter planes. The technology of planes improved quickly. Engines became lighter in weight but more powerful. Aircraft frames became lighter but stronger. So planes became faster and easier to control. Most fighters had only one seat, so the pilot both flew the plane and fired the guns.

The Fokker Dr. 1

Most planes were **biplanes**. They had two sets of wings, one above the other, linked by **struts** and wires. This made a strong box-like structure. There were also triplanes, with three sets of wings. The most famous triplane was the Fokker Dr. 1, flown by the famous German fighter pilot Manfred von Richthofen (also known as the Red Baron). The plane could turn tightly and climb steeply, and it was one of the best fighters of World War I.

Firing Through the Propeller

The first single-seat planes had guns mounted on the wing above the cockpit, so that bullets missed the spinning propeller. But the best place for a gun to be placed in a single-seat fighter was in front of the cockpit, where the pilot could look along it to aim, and where he could reach it in case it jammed. So engineers invented interrupter gear or synchro gear, which stopped the gun from firing if a propeller blade was in the path of a bullet.

The Chandelle:
turning 180
degrees while
climbing steeply

The spin: diving and rolling
to lose altitude quickly ·····················

The half roll:
rolling then diving
to turn back

Dogfight Tricks

Combat pilots fought each other in dogfights, making
their planes dive, roll, and turn to try to get into
position to attack or to escape from an attacker.
Pilots invented attacking and defensive moves.

Eddie Rickenbacker

Life as a World War I pilot was dangerous. Many pilots were
shot down after only a few flights. But some were
very successful and shot down dozens of enemy planes.
Among these fighter **aces** was US pilot Eddie Rickenbacker.
He shot down twenty-six planes and lived to tell the tale.

BATTLE OF BRITAIN FIGHTERS

The Battle of Britain was a fight for command of the skies over Britain in the summer of 1940, during World War II (1939-1945). The Luftwaffe (German air force) sent bombers to attack British ships, airfields, and factories. British fighters tried to stop the bombers from reaching their targets, and German fighters tried to protect the bombers.

SUPERMARINE SPITFIRE

Length: 30 feet (9.1 m)

Wingspan: 37 feet (11.2 m)

Weight: 2.5 tons (2.3 metric tons)

Engine: Rolls-Royce Merlin or Griffin

Top speed: 370 miles (595 km) per hour

Top height: 36,499 feet (11,125 m)

Weapons: Hispano cannon / Browning machine gun

Number built: 20,351

First flight: March 1936

Supermarine Spitfire

By the time World War II began, most fighters were made of metal, were **monoplanes**, and had **in-line engines** or **radial engines** instead of rotary engines. The Supermarine Spitfire could climb high, powered by its Rolls-Royce Merlin or Griffin engine. It was armed with cannons in the wings that fired explosive shells.

Cockpit Controls

A glass canopy protected a Spitfire's cockpit from the wind and cold. There were controls to steer the plane through the air and to work the engine and other parts. Instruments showed the plane's speed, **altitude**, and fuel level.

throttle controlled engine power

altimeter showed height above ground

air speed indicator

trigger for cannons

control stick made the nose go up or down and made the plane roll

rudder pedals made the plane turn from side to side

Messerschmitt Bf 109

The Bf 109 was Germany's best World War II fighter, closely matching the **Allies'** Spitfire. It had an all-metal body and a foldaway undercarriage. Nearly 34,000 were built. The aircraft played a big role in Germany's early victories and could be both a fighter and a ground-attack machine.

P-51 MUSTANG

The Mustang joined World War II late, but it played an important role in the victory for Britain, the United States, and their allies. This American single-seat fighter was one of the war's most advanced aircraft. In Europe it defended American bombers against German fighters on long-**range** raids over Germany and attacked German airfields. In the Pacific it took on Japan's Mitsubishi A6M Zero.

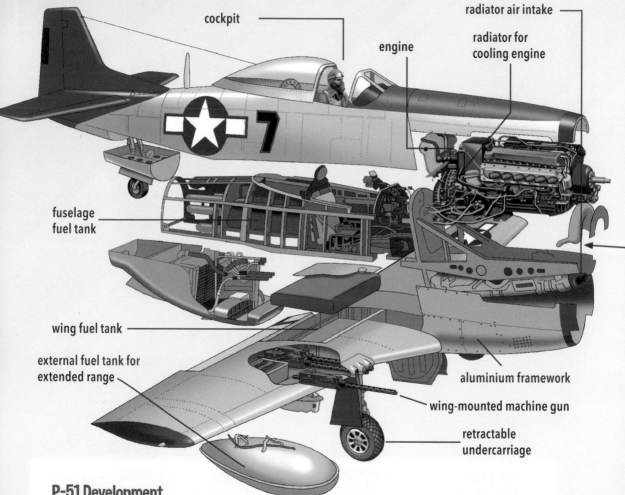

cockpit

engine

radiator air intake

radiator for cooling engine

fuselage fuel tank

wing fuel tank

external fuel tank for extended range

aluminium framework

wing-mounted machine gun

retractable undercarriage

P-51 Development

The P-51 Mustang was built by North American Aviation. It was first developed for Britain's Royal Air Force (RAF), which needed fighters early in the war. The prototype first flew in October 1940. Its main features were a thin, efficient wing, a smooth fuselage with low **drag**, and an all-aluminium frame and skin. It could also carry fuel tanks on its wings to improve its range. The first Mustang entered service with the RAF in January 1942. It served with the US Air Force until the early 1950s.

Formation

Fighters such as the Mustang flew together in small groups. This was called flying in formation. Pilots in formation could keep an eye on one another and defend one another in case they were attacked.

— propeller

P-51 MUSTANG

Length: 32 feet (9.8 m)

Wingspan: 37 feet (11.3 m)

Weight: 3.9 tons (3.5 metric tons)

Engine: Packard V-12

Top speed: 440 miles (708 km) per hour

Top height: 41,995 feet (12,800 m)

Weapons: 6 Browning machine guns /rockets

Number built: more than 15,000

First flight: October 1940

Recording Kills

Fighter pilots would paint symbols on their planes to show how many enemy planes they had shot down. The pilot of this Mustang has claimed eight German kills. Mustang pilots claimed to have shot down nearly five thousand enemy planes during World War II.

FIRST JET FIGHTERS

Until the 1930s, all fighter planes were powered by propellers turned by engines that had pistons moving up and down in cylinders (which work like the engines on cars). But propeller-driven planes can't fly at very high altitudes where the air is thin, and they can't fly superfast. Jet-powered planes can fly both high and fast, so the invention of the jet engine in the 1930s in Germany and England was an important step in the development of fighter planes.

Extra Thrust

Afterburners boost the power of a fighter's jet engines. They squirt fuel into the hot gases in the exhaust, creating more hot gases. Afterburners allow for quick takeoffs and fast climbs.

MESSERSCHMITT ME 262

The German Me 262 was the first jet-powered fighter to go into battle. It first flew in 1942 during World War II, but it didn't enter service until 1944 because of problems with its new jet engines. The Me 262 was successful at attacking Allied bombers, but it came too late to make a difference.

ME 262

Length: 35 feet (10.6 m)

Wingspan: 41 feet (12.6 m)

Weight: 4.2 tons (3.8 metric tons)

Engines: Twin Junkers Jumo 004 turbojets

Top speed: 559 miles (900 km) per hour

Top height: 37,566 feet (11,450 m)

Weapons: four 30 mm cannons, twenty-four rockets

Number built: 1,430

First flight: July 1942

Number of kills: 542

JET ENGINE

A jet engine works by sending a fast-moving jet of hot gases from its exhaust nozzle. This pushes the plane forward.

fuel burns in combustion chamber

compressor squeezes air

air intake

turbojet engine

11

turbine turns the compressor

hot gases stream out of nozzle

hot gases turn the turbine

STEALTHY MACHINES

Many modern fighters, such as the Lockheed Martin F-22 Raptor and the Lockheed Martin F-35 Lightning, feature stealth technology. This technology makes it more difficult for a fighter to be detected by sensors such as **radar** sensors and heat sensors. Ground defenses, other aircraft, and homing missiles use these sensors to detect, track, and attack fighter aircraft. Being stealthy allows fighters to reach their targets without being spotted and attacked.

Lockheed F-117A Nighthawk

The amazing angular design of the Lockheed F-117A remained top secret for many years. This was the world's first fighter to have stealth technology, and it was nicknamed the Stealth Fighter.

The F-117A made its first flight in 1981 and started operating with the US Air Force in 1983. It flew many missions during the Iraq War of 1991 and finally retired from service in 2008. The F-117's odd shape made it too tricky for pilots to control by hand, so it was flown using a computer.

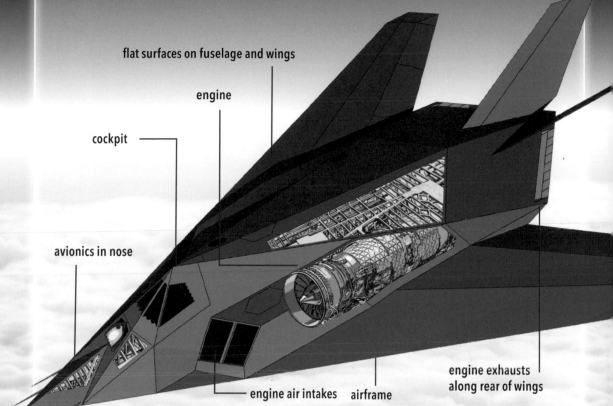

flat surfaces on fuselage and wings

engine

cockpit

avionics in nose

engine air intakes   airframe

engine exhausts
along rear of wings

Stealth Tricks

The fuselage and wings of the F-117A were divided into flat panels to make the plane almost invisible to radar. When radar waves hit the F-117, they bounced off, but hardly ever back toward the radar detector. The aircraft also had radar-absorbing paint to reduce the number of waves that bounced off. The engine nozzles were designed to hide the hot engine exhaust that could give away the plane's position to heat sensors.

F-117A

Length:	66 feet (20.1 m)
Wingspan:	43 feet (13.2 m)
Weight:	15 tons (13.4 metric tons)
Engines:	Twin General Electric turbofans
Top speed:	617 miles (993 km) per hour
Top height:	45,000 feet (13,716 m)
Weapons:	20 mm cannon, missiles
Number built:	64
First flight:	June 1981

AT THE CONTROLS

Taking the controls of a state-of-the-art fighter plane is a dream for many pilots. Fighter pilots must be great at flying, often at high speeds and low to the ground. But they must also be able to process massive amounts of information coming from their aircraft's systems and to think fast and make quick decisions to complete their missions safely. This all takes years of training.

In the Cockpit

The controls of a modern fighter are fly-by-wire or fly-by-light. The pilot steers the plane, but a computer controls it using electronic or light signals. Navigation instruments show the terrain below, even when it's cloudy. Weapons systems detect, track, and target enemy aircraft and ground targets.

Flying Suit and Helmet

During high-speed turns, pilots experience an effect called high-g. This causes blood to drain from the head to the legs, which can lead to blackouts. To prevent this, pilots wear a g-suit, which squeezes their legs to keep too much blood from flowing into them. The helmet contains headphones, a microphone, and sometimes a computer display and sensors that track where the pilot is looking.

Pilot is released from the seat to parachute to the ground

Parachute opens

Rockets propel the seat away from the plane

Canopy is blown off, then a catapult fires the seat up and out

Ejector Seat

The pilot's seat can be a lifesaver. In an emergency, if the pilot thinks the aircraft is going to crash, he or she pulls a handle on the seat, and the seat is blasted out of the cockpit with the pilot still strapped in.

Simulator

A flight simulator recreates what it is like to fly an aircraft, but without the danger. The simulator creates the world outside the cockpit using computer graphics, and twists and rolls the cockpit around with hydraulics. Fighter pilots learn to fly particular fighters (this simulator is for an F-16 Flying Falcon) using simulators. They also practice how to deal with emergency situations and use new weapons.

TARGETING WEAPONS

Fighter planes would be useless without their weapons. Most modern fighters are multirole aircraft, which means they can be fighters, fighter-bombers, or ground-attack aircraft. Fighters can carry several different weapons for attacking different targets. These weapons include cannons and antiaircraft missiles for attacking other aircraft, ground-attack missiles for destroying tanks, and rockets and **laser**-guided bombs. They sometimes also carry antiship missiles.

Firing a Missile

A missile is a self-propelled weapon that is guided to its target. It has a rocket motor that pushes it along. Different guidance systems use lasers, radar, and infrared light to guide missiles. The guidance system can be on the aircraft (called remote guidance) or on the missile itself (called homing guidance). For example, in an infrared homing missile (also called a heat-seeking missile), the missile detects heat from its target and keeps adjusting its steering fins so that it is traveling toward the heat source.

Night Sights

At night, pilots pick out their targets using a night sight, also known as an image intensifier. This system uses an infrared camera, which forms a picture using the heat coming from objects on the ground. Hotter objects appear brighter in the image. The images appear on cockpit screens or a display inside the pilot's helmet.

Sukhoi Su-34

Weapons Pylons

Most missiles are carried under a fighter's wings, in places called weapons stations (*shown left on a Sukhoi Su-34*). At each station there is a connector called a pylon, and each pylon holds a particular weapon. The weapons are locked to the pylons until they are fired. Pylons and weapons can be changed so that the fighter can attack different sorts of targets on different missions.

ATTACK HELICOPTERS

Attack helicopters, also known as helicopter gunships, such as the Boeing Apache and
Mil Mi-24, have deadly firepower. They carry out attacks on targets on the ground.
Helicopters can hover close to their targets and operate from bases without runways.
They carry similar weapons to fighter planes but also have powerful machine guns.

Boeing AH-64D Apache Longbow

This twin-engined attack helicopter's main role is to destroy enemy weapons such as tanks and mobile guns. The pilot sits in the front cockpit, and the copilot (who is also the gunner) sits in the rear cockpit, above and behind the pilot. The Apache carries rockets, and its powerful machine gun can be "slaved" to the gunner's helmet. This means it is aimed by movements of the gunner's head. Apache pilots fly low, using hills and valleys for cover. The tactic is known as terrain masking.

Apache AH-64

Length: 58 feet (17.7 m)

Rotor diameter: 48 feet (14.6 m)

Weight: 5.7 tons (5.2 metric tons)

Engines: Twin General Electric turboshafts

Top speed: 182 miles (293 km) per hour

Top height: 20,997 feet (6,400 m)

Weapons: machine gun, missiles, rockets

Number built: more than 2,000

First flight: September 1975

Flares for Defense

Attack helicopters are in danger of attack from missiles fired from aircraft and the ground. If a helicopter is targeted by heat-seeking missiles, the pilots can send out flares to confuse the missile. These helicopters can also pull off radical moves if needed.

F-35 FIGHTER

The Lockheed Martin F–35 Lightning is a fifth generation fighter jet (each major advance in fighter technology brings in a new generation of fighter jet). It is one of the most modern fighters, featuring stealth technology, fly-by-wire controls, advanced digital **avionics**, an array of sensors, and high-speed communications. It is very agile but can also fly at supersonic speeds.

engine

lift fan door

ejection seat

lift fan

drive shaft from engine

radar

Engine Nozzle
During forward flight, the rear engine exhaust points backward. The lift fan duct is closed to give the fuselage a smooth shape.

control surfaces
used to tilt and
roll the jet

Multiple Roles

The F-35 has been designed to perform many different jobs. There are three main models:

F-35A

This is a high-performance multirole fighter. It is a conventional takeoff and landing (CTOL) aircraft, which operates from airbases with runways.

F-35B

The F-35B is a short takeoff and vertical landing (STOVL) aircraft. It needs only a short runway for takeoff and can land vertically. It operates from small bases and from the decks of aircraft carriers.

engine nozzle
tilts down for
STOVL

F-35C

This model is designed for taking off and landing on the restricted flight decks of aircraft carriers, and it has a strengthened undercarriage for hard landings. It is a long-range strike fighter, for attacking ground targets.

roll nozzle

STOVL Operations

For short takeoffs and for vertical landings, the F-35B has a lift fan behind the cockpit. A door above the fan opens, and the fan is connected to the engine. The fan forces air down, pushing the plane up. At the same time, the engine exhaust tilts downward, adding to the upward push. After takeoff, the engine exhaust points backward, the fan switches off, and the F-35B starts to fly forward, using its wings for lift.

TIMELINE

1903
The Wright Brothers perform the first controlled, powered flight with their plane Flyer.

1917
The Fokker Dr. 1, a German triplane, makes it first flight.

1936
The Supermarine Spitfire makes its first flight.

1939
World War II begins.

1942
The Messerschmitt Me 262 becomes the first jet fighter.

1945
World War II ends.

1961
The last Spitfire retires from duty.

1918
The fighter ace Baron Manfred von Richthofen is killed in combat.

1937
The first jet engine is developed.

1942
The P-51 Mustang takes off for the first time.

1935
The Messerschmitt Bf 109 makes its first flight.

1940
British and German planes fight in the Battle of Britain.

1915
The Airco DH. 2 pusher plane makes its first flight.

1914
World War I begins and countries start to build fighter planes.

1974
The General Dynamics F-16 becomes the first fighter to take off with fly-by-wire controls.

1986
The Apache AH-64 attack helicopter enters service with the US Army.

2006
The Lockheed Martin F-35 makes its first test flight.

1981
The F-117A Nighthawk stealth fighter makes its first flight.

FACT FILE

One of World War II's best fighters, the De Havilland Mosquito, was made entirely from wood.

The gunner of the Apache AH-64 has a special helmet linked to the helicopter's gun. The gun aims where the gunner looks.

During World War I, Manfred von Richthofen led a group of German pilots known as the Flying Circus. Von Richthofen alone shot down eighty aircraft before he was killed in 1918.

In 1944, Germany built a rocket-powered fighter: the Messerschmitt 163 Komet. This tiny plane could fly at more than 621 miles (1,000 km) per hour.

The life expectancy of a Spitfire pilot who fought in the Battle of Britain was just four weeks.

The engine of an F-35 produces enough push to lift a 22-ton (20 metric tons) weight.

The Lockheed F-117A first flew in 1981, but its existence was kept top secret until 1988.

The Mustang carried enough fuel to allow it to fly from Britain to Germany and back to protect bombers on bombing raids.

GLOSSARY

ace: a fighter pilot who shoots down many enemy planes

air superiority: having control of the air over a battlefield so that enemy planes can't fly

air-to-air: weapons fired from a plane in the air to attack a target also in the air

air-to-ground: weapons fired from a plane in the air to attack a target on the ground

Allies: the combined forces of Britain, the United States, and other countries during World War I and World War II

altitude: the distance that a plane is above sea level

avionics: short for aviation electronics, all the electronics needed for flying and navigating a modern plane

biplane: a plane with two pairs of wings, one above the other

drag: the resistance the air makes on a plane as the plane flies through the air

fuselage: the main body of an aicraft

in-line engine: an engine in which the cylinders are arranged in a line

laser: an intense beam of light

monoplane: a plane with just one pair of wings. Most modern planes are monoplanes.

radar: a device that detects objects by sending out radio waves and sensing them bounce back

radial engine: an engine in which the cylinders are arranged in a circle

range: the maximum distance that an aircraft can fly before getting short on fuel

rotary engine: an engine in which the cylinders are arranged in a circle and rotate with the propeller

Eddie Rickenbacker, World War I pilot

stealthy: an aircraft with stealth technology, which makes it difficult to detect

strut: a rigid rod that keeps parts of a structure in place

triplane: a plane with three pairs of wings, one above the other

wingspan: the distance from one wing tip to the other on a plane

Wreckage of a World War I German Albatross fighter biplane—its pilots were advised not to perform steep dives because its wings had a tendency to develop cracks and fail

An air-to-air missile attached under the wing of a Russian fighter plane

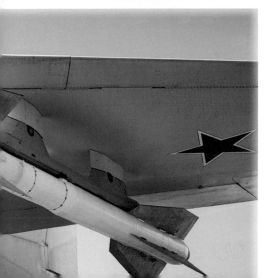

INDEX

The Author

Chris Oxlade is an experienced author of educational books for children with more than two hundred titles to his name, including many on science and technology. He enjoys camping and adventurous outdoor sports, including rock climbing, hill running, kayaking, and sailing. He lives in England with his wife, children, and dogs.

Picture Credits (abbreviations: t = top; b = bottom; c = center; l = left; r = right)
© www.shutterstock.com: 1bc, 2bl, 4c, 12c, 20l, 29tr, 30-31bc, 31tr.
3, c = KEYSTONE Pictures USA / Alamy Stock Photo. 6-7, c = US Air Force Photo / Alamy Stock Photo.
7, t = Andrew Harker / Alamy Stock Photo. 8, c = Angus McComiskey / Alamy Stock Photo. 9, t = Peter
Wheeler / Alamy Stock Photo. 9, c = Ian Dagnall / Alamy Stock Photo. 9, b = World History Archive /
Alamy Stock Photo. 10, b = Real Window Gallery / Alamy Stock Photo. 10-11, c = Antony Nettle / Alamy
Stock Photo. 11, b = The Granger Collection / Alamy Stock Photo. 13, t = Trinity Mirror / Mirrorpix /
Alamy Stock Photo. 13, b = Antony Nettle / Alamy Stock Photo. 15, t = Antony Nettle / Alamy Stock
Photo. 15, b = CBW / Alamy Stock Photo. 16, b = Stocktrek Images, Inc. / Alamy Stock Photo. 16-17, c
= age fotostock / Alamy Stock Photo. 18-19, c = age fotostock / Alamy Stock Photo. 21, cl = A. T. Willet
/ Alamy Stock Photo. 21, b = US Airforce Photo / Alamy Stock Photo. 22-23, c = Stocktrek Images, Inc. /
Alamy Stock Photo. 23, t = PhotoEdit / Alamy Stock Photo. 23, b = Stocktrek Images, Inc. /Alamy Stock
Photo. 24-25, c = robert Leyland / Alamy Stock Photo. 26, b = Mint Photography / Alamy Stock Photo.
27, b = Lockheed Martin. 29, b = Granger Historical Picture Archive / Alamy Stock Photo.